21

RIVER FOREST PUBLIC LIBRARY
735 Lathrop Avenue
River Forest, Illinois 60305
708 / 366-5205

12/07

WORLD OF
INSECTS

BUTTERFLIES

by Sophie Lockwood

Content Adviser: Michael Breed, Ph.D., Professor,
Ecology and Evolutionary Biology,
The University of Colorado, Boulder

THE CHILD'S WORLD®, MANKATO, MINNESOTA

Butterflies

Published in the United States of America by The Child's World®
1980 Lookout Drive • Mankato, MN 56003-1705
800-599-READ • www.childsworld.com

Acknowledgements:

The Child's World®: Mary Berendes, Publishing Director

The Creative Spark: Mary Francis, Project Director; Wendy Mead, Editor; Deborah Goodsite, Photo Researcher

The Design Lab: Kathleen Petelinsek, Designer, Production Artist, and Cartographer

Photos:

Cover: Mike Bentley/iStockphoto.com; frontispiece: E. R. Degginger/Photo Researchers, Inc.; half title and CIP: Mike Bentley/iStockphoto.com.

Interior: Animals Animals/Earth Scenes: 16–17 (J.A.L. Cooke/OSF), 5, 31 (Donald Specker); Oxford Scientific: 5, 34 (Patti Murray /Animals Animals/Earth Scenes); iStockphoto.com: 5, 9 (Graham Prentice), 25 (Nicholas Cacchione), 5, 27 (Dan Wood), 22–23 (tcp); Landov: 36 (Wolfgang Thieme/DPA); Minden Pictures: 10 (Frans Lanting), 12–13, 19 (Hans Christoph Kappel/npl); Nativestock.com: 29 (Marilyn Angel Wynn); Visuals Unlimited: 5, 15 (Leroy Simon), 21 (Kjell B. Sandved), 33 (Ross Frid).

Map: The Design Lab: 7.

Library of Congress Cataloging-in-Publication Data

Lockwood, Sophie.
 Butterflies / by Sophie Lockwood.
   p. cm.—(The world of insects)
 Includes index.
 ISBN-13: 978-1-59296-820-6 (library bound: alk. paper)
 ISBN-10: 1-59296-820-1 (library bound: alk. paper)
 1. Butterflies—Juvenile literature. I. Title.
 QL544.2.L65 2007
 595.78'9—dc22   2006103458

TABLE OF CONTENTS

Chapter One

A Flutter of Orange and Black

It is early spring in the mountains of central Mexico. In a quiet pine grove, orange-and-black butterflies blanket every branch and every needle of every tree. These brilliantly colored monarch butterflies have spent the winter motionless, clinging to their perches. Now, warmer weather sends a message to these sluggish sleepers. Wings flutter, looking much like stained-glass windows.

Males and females head to milkweed meadows. They mate, and the females lay their eggs on the underside of milkweed leaves. The eggs hatch in three to fifteen days, depending on the weather. White, black, and orange-striped caterpillars emerge and act like non-stop eating machines. In two weeks, the **larvae** grow to 5 centimeters (2 inches) long. Inside their bodies, a change is taking place. This change signals the time for wormlike caterpillars to transform into butterflies.

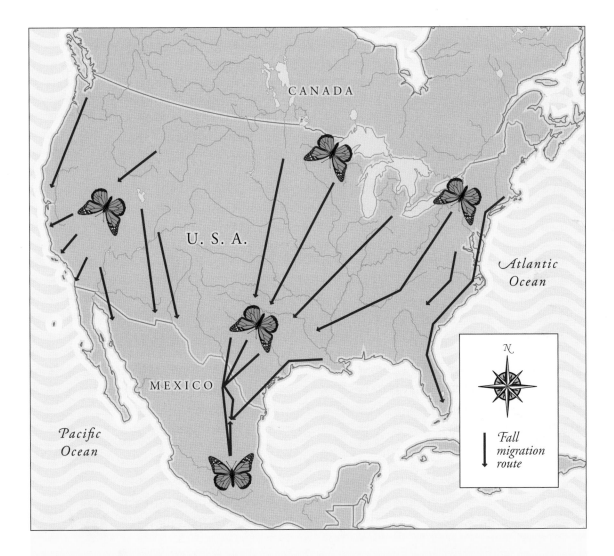

Each caterpillar attaches its body to a milkweed branch. It sheds its skin and forms a waxy, jade green **chrysalis**. Within the chrysalis, a remarkable change takes place. In two or three weeks, the ugly caterpillar becomes a beautiful monarch butterfly.

This map shows the migration paths of monarch butterflies.

While the **metamorphosis** from caterpillar to butterfly is remarkable, it is not the most interesting aspect of monarchs. What has amazed humans for hundreds of years is the monarchs' incredible migration.

The new Mexican monarchs wings are crumpled and soft. When they emerge, the butterflies inflate their wings by pumping them full of blood from its stomach. They must wait for the wings to stiffen and dry. Then the monarchs take flight, heading northward to yet another milkweed meadow. In all, it takes three or four generations of monarchs to finish their migration. Each generation's adults travel a part of the migratory path to the northern United States or southern Canada. Adults survive only a few weeks—just as long as it takes to reach a new milkweed meadow and mate.

The last monarch generation of the season is different from all the others. This generation has little interest in mating and has a basic need to travel. Their destination is programmed into their brains. It's like they have their own automatic mapping system. Although these particular butterflies have never been to Mexico, they know exactly where to go. It takes weeks for them to make their way to the pine groves west of Mexico City, and yet they never get lost.

In Mexico, the butterflies settle on the pines, becoming motionless. This generation of monarchs has two goals. They need to survive and save energy. While other generations of monarchs live only a few weeks, these wintering butterflies must survive much longer. They must live from autumn to the following spring to prevent the species from coming to an end.

A monarch butterfly emerges from its chrysalis.

Did You Know?
In Mexico, the monarchs arrive in November, a time when many Mexicans are celebrating a religious holiday connected to the butterflies. This tradition dates back to the days before Columbus arrived in the New World. The people believe that the butterflies represent the souls of the dead returning home.

What a miraculous journey! Several generations of butterflies make a round trip of more than 3,200 kilometers (2,000 miles) with no previous experience. They follow the path by instinct, a pattern of behavior they are born with.

Monarch butterflies rest in their winter home in Mexico.

Chapter Two

The Butterfly Cycle of Life

Butterflies may be nature's most beautiful creatures. They come in a rainbow of colors from deep, rich purples to brilliant blues and vivid yellows. Their bodies are thin. Their wings are delicate. They are the stars of the insect world.

BODY PARTS

A butterfly consists of a three-part body, six legs, and four wings. The body has a head, a **thorax**, and an **abdomen**. Depending on the species, all six legs may be usable or the two front legs may be short and useless.

A butterfly's head features a set of compound eyes, **antennae**, and a **proboscis**. It has a brain about the size of this dot: •. The eyes are shaped like balls, each with thousands of six-sided **facets**, called **ommatidia**. Butterfly eyes see everything as a blur, but can identify size, shape, movement, and a range of colors including ultraviolet light. The

antennae

head

wings   wings

thorax

abdomen

A large tortoiseshell butterfly, like all butterflies, has three main body parts.

human eye can see a range of light from violet to red, or the colors of a rainbow. Ultraviolet light is beyond the range of human eyesight. Butterflies use their eyes to spot predators, find food, and, most importantly, locate the perfect mate.

Butterfly antennae are highly sensitive and allow the insect to feel, smell, and maintain balance. Butterfly antennae usually have small clubs on the ends. At the base of the antennae, the Johnston's organ helps the butterfly maintain balance and course during flight. This organ is a collection of cells that an insect uses to sense location when flying.

The proboscis is a long tube used like a tongue to suck liquids. Most butterflies drink flower nectar, animal urine, body fluids, and the liquid of rotten fruit. On either side of the proboscis are palps, which are stubby parts similar to antennae. The palps are used to taste whether an item is food or not.

The thorax or chest is the middle section of a butterfly's body, and the center of movement. Three pairs of legs attach to the thorax. Each leg is jointed, with the tips acting as taste organs. A butterfly needs strong muscles in the thorax to allow it to fly. During flight, the wings of most butterflies move in a figure-eight fashion, allowing it to swim or float in the air. The wings and outer shell of the body are made of chitin, a protein substance similar to fingernails.

The abdomen contains most of a butterfly's major body organs. The abdomen is soft and made up of ten sections. The abdomen contains **reproductive** organs, digestive organs, and organs to remove waste products. A flexible, tubelike heart pumps transparent blood through the body and wings. Butterflies breathe through tiny holes, called **spiracles**, on either side of the abdomen. They don't have lungs.

REPRODUCTION

The life cycle of the butterfly is an excellent example of complete metamorphosis. The butterfly's life begins in the egg stage. The egg develops into a larva and then a **pupa**. It transforms finally into an adult butterfly called an imago.

Adult butterflies have an irresistible need to mate. Males and females seek mates almost immediately after emerging from the pupae cases. A female attracts males in two different ways. Some females emit a chemical scent called a **pheromone** into the air. Willing males from

miles around try to mate with the female. Other females attract mates by using visual signals. They send signals through their flight patterns. The scales on their wings reflect ultraviolet light, which draws males near. The problem with visual signals is that the males must be able to see the females to get the message. The males provide the sperm, and the eggs are fertilized as the females lay them.

A Chinese yellow swallowtail caterpillar inches along a leaf.

A cabbage butterfly larva emerges from an egg.

Each female deposits a different number of eggs. Most female monarch butterflies lay about 100 eggs. With luck, two of those eggs will survive to become healthy adult butterflies. The others will be lost to bad weather, viruses, bacteria, or predators. Some females carefully deposit each egg with their **ovipositors**. Other females spread their eggs the same way a person would spread wildflower seeds. The number of eggs depends on the species and how safe the eggs are once laid.

Eggs come in a variety of shapes, sizes, and shades. They may be perfectly round or oval-shaped. Colors include green, white, or yellow, and most are the same shade as the leaves, bark, or flowers on which they have been deposited. The egg develops much as a bird's egg, the yolk providing food for the larva developing inside.

Usually, the eggs are laid on their favorite food source. Within a week, the egg darkens, and a tiny larva appears. It immediately eats its first meal—its own eggshell. From then on, larvae eat with an endless appetite and grow accordingly. As the cater-pillar grows, it sheds its **exoskeleton**, or its outer shell, each time it needs to enlarge its body. Each

Who Said That?
William Wordsworth wrote a poem about these amazing insects called "To a Butterfly." Here are a few lines of the poet's work:
I've watched you now a full half-hour,
Self-poised upon that yellow flower;
And, little Butterfly! indeed
I know not if you sleep or feed.
Visit your local library to read the complete poem and other poems by the author.

stage of caterpillar development is called an instar, and butterfly larvae go through several instars as they develop.

The job of larvae is to eat and grow. Once they reach a certain size, caterpillars automatically prepare for their next stage of life. They enter the pupa stage. The outside of the caterpillar hardens into a chrysalis. This outer shell is an exoskeleton, serving as a protective case.

The caterpillar oozes a thin strand of silk to hold the chrysalis in place. When the pupa stage is in action, the caterpillar's body parts are basically rearranged to become a butterfly. Wings develop, legs lengthen, and color changes inside the chrysalis.

After two or three weeks, a full-grown butterfly emerges. Its wings are wrinkly and soft. The butterfly hangs upside-down, pumping blood into its wings and waiting for the wings to open fully and harden. Once the wings are firm, the adult butterfly tests its wings and takes off. The cycle of life begins again as soon as a male and female mate.

During each stage of development—egg, larva, pupa, and adult—butterflies are tasty morsels for many predators. Dozens of species, particularly spiders, flies, wasps, and beetles, feed on eggs, caterpillars, or pupae. Birds feast on all stages of butterflies, as do snakes, lizards, dragonflies, and praying mantis.

A caterpillar becomes a butterfly after a few weeks inside a chrysalis.

Chapter Three

Butterflies and More Butterflies

Butterflies and moths belong to the order *Lepidoptera,* a huge insect order with nearly 200,000 species. Between 18,000 and 20,000 species of *Lepidoptera* are butterflies. The name *Lepidoptera* is Greek for "scaly wings." Each wing is covered with layers of scales. The scales are small but can be seen easily under a microscope. Brush a finger against a butterfly wing, and that finger comes away with a fine coat of dust. That dust is really scales.

Butterflies are basically good-looking moths, although there are some fairly plain-looking butterflies and some rather attractive moths. The differences between butterflies and moths are few and refer to "most," but not "all" species. Most butterflies are day fliers, while moths fly at night. All butterflies have a proboscis, but some moths do not. Butterflies rest their wings up against each other, while moths fold their wings down over their backs. A butterfly larva

forms a chrysalis, while a moth larva spins a cocoon. Many butterflies have clubs on the end of their antennae. Moths have feathery antennae ends.

NATURAL DEFENSES

Butterflies seem to be defenseless. They do not have fangs or claws. Instead butterflies taste so bad that no creature wants to take a bite. Butterfly caterpillars use some strange techniques to fend off predators. Swallowtail butterfly larvae look remarkably

Did You Know?
The fastest flying butterflies are skippers, so named because they flit from one flower to another. The regent skipper, *Euschemon rafflesia* can fly at 60 kilometers (37 miles) per hour.

A close-up photograph shows the scales found on a butterfly's wing.

You can see how much this Indian leaf butterfly looks like a dead leaf!

like bird droppings. Others, like monarch caterpillars, feed on toxic plants and retain that toxin in their systems. They taste horrible, and few predators want to eat them. Some caterpillars grow hideous sharp spines that keep predators away.

Butterfly pupae are exposed to many predators, yet the pupae also have protective cases and colorations. The pupa of an owl butterfly **mimics** a brown, dead leaf, and the morpho butterfly's chrysalis looks surprisingly like a small green pepper.

Distinctive coloring and a foul taste provide the best defenses for adult butterflies. When an Indian leaf butterfly closes its wings, it blends in so well with dead leaves that even the most observant human cannot tell leaf from insect. Sometimes color sends a false message—the viceroy butterfly wears the same colors as the monarch but is not poisonous. Still, birds that shy away from foul-tasting monarchs avoid viceroys, just in case. Eyespots provide some species with another trick. The eyespots on the owl butterfly look incredibly like the eyes of predatory birds and help scare away other animals.

Trailing tails can also be a handy trick. Thin projections from the hind wings give the impression of antennae or even a false head. The *Hypolycaena liara* of Uganda and many swallowtails have long, hanging hind wings. Predators pounce and get a bite of wing, but the butterfly itself flits away safely. In the wild, many swallowtails have bits of their hind wings missing from just such an attack.

MAJOR BUTTERFLY SUPERFAMILIES

Butterflies have far fewer species than moths and far fewer superfamilies, large groups of butterflies with similar characteristics. These families include the skippers (Hesperidae) and the true butterflies (Papilionidae, Pieridae, Nymphalidae, and Lycaenidae).

The Hesperidae (hes-PAIR-ih-dee) has about 3,500 member species. Many bear the common name of skipper and look more like moths than butterflies. Skippers are quick-flying butterflies that flit from flower to flower. They have stout bodies, large heads, and fairly dull coloring. A typical hesperid butterfly is the regent skipper with bright black and yellow

wing coloring and a brilliant red-tipped abdomen. The wings of the regent skipper are joined by a coupling hook, much like the wings of moths.

The Papilionidae (pah-pihl-ee-AHN-ih-dee) contains many of the beauties of the butterfly world, including birdwings, swallowtails, and stunning festoons. The Queen Alexandra's birdwing belongs to the giant butterfly subspecies, mostly found in the tropics. Swallowtails have graceful wings and vivid colors. Among the most beautiful are the checkered swallowtail with its delicate, lacy coloring, and the tiger swallowtail with bright yellow and

The distinctive long "tails" on its wings help identify this butterfly as a tiger swallowtail.

black-brown stripes. The Spanish festoon is a checkered butterfly known for its mix of brown, white, and red markings and attractive scalloped wing edges.

Pieridae (PEER-ih-dee) is the official name for butterflies commonly referred to as whites, yellows, or sulfurs. The coloring comes from the butterfly's bodily waste products. The most unique pierid butterfly is the orange albatross, the only fully orange butterfly in the world. More interesting is the California dogface, with a yellow "dog's face" in the forewing coloring. More common than the dogface species is the cabbage butterfly, found in many backyard gardens.

Butterflies that are part of the Nymphalidae (nihm-FAHL-ih-dee) number nearly 5,000. They include various emperors, monarchs, fritillaries, and admirals. They are characterized by having undeveloped front legs. The loveliest nymphalid butterfly is the common map, so named for its strangely patterned markings. The brilliant blue morpho butterflies have the most stunning blue colors—shades achieved by drinking the salts found in animal urine.

Another large 5,000-member family is Lycaenidae (lye-SEEN-ih-dee). These are species of small, bright-colored butterflies, including the hairstreaks, metalmarks, and

blues. Hewitson's blue hairstreak features a rich blue hue with fearsome eyespots on the hind wing tails. Many butterflies have brilliantly colored upper wings and dull, **camouflage** on their underwings. The unusual fiery jewel is just the opposite. Its upper wings are brown with blue or violet markings. Its underside is fiery red and bright blue.

The morpho blue butterfly gets its color from what it drinks.

Chapter Four

In Appreciation of Butterflies

The Shoshone people tell the legend of the Ladies' Fancy Shawl Dance. Many years ago, a beautiful butterfly lost her mate and was overwhelmed with grief. She wrapped her beauty in a dull-colored cocoon to show her sadness. She did not sleep or eat, and she felt terribly restless.

Realizing she needed a change in her life, she packed her belongings and headed on a long, sorrowful journey. As she traveled, she saw many sights but none healed her heart until she came upon a truly beautiful stone. She threw away the dull cocoon and put on her beautiful butterfly wings again. Her feet danced, moving in a complicated pattern that expressed great joy.

Today, many Shoshone still celebrate the Ladies' Fancy Shawl Dance, the dance of the butterflies. The complicated steps and swirling moves represent a butterfly's flight pattern.

In many cultures, the butterfly is a symbol of beauty, life, and change. No other creature experiences as dramatic a change from the sluglike caterpillar to the lush beauty of an adult butterfly. In mythology, butterflies symbolize the journey of a spirit from one life to the next. For some, this is the trip that represents freedom of the spirit after death. For others, the end of one life is rebirth into the next life. The last breath a dying person takes, in some myths, comes out as a butterfly. In Asia, when butterflies come together, they are the spirits of lovers separated by death. As the butterflies meet, the lovers are reunited.

The Shoshone celebrate the butterfly with the Ladies' Fancy Shawl Dance.

Would You Believe?
The Irish offer this blessing to their loved ones:
> *May the wings of the butterfly*
> *kiss the sun*
> *And find your shoulder to light on*
> *To bring you luck, happiness,*
> *and riches*
> *Today, tomorrow, and beyond.*

Some Native American legends claim that one should tell a wish to a butterfly, then set it free. The Great Spirit will be pleased and grant the wish. Other native tales claim that the Great Spirit collected the most beautiful colors—blues of sky and lake, yellow of the sun, black from a young woman's hair—and made them butterflies.

Butterfly colors can be considered omens of the future. White butterflies mean good luck. Yellow ones say good weather is on the way. Red butterflies tell of good health, while a butterfly seen flying at night means sickness in the future. On the other hand, a butterfly flitting in one's house says someone will soon be married. The Zuni Indians claim that when a white butterfly comes, so does summer. They also believe that a white butterfly coming from the southwest brings rain.

CREEPY CUISINE

In certain parts of the world, millions of people eat caterpillars. This is not a trendy snack or a passing fad. Caterpillars contain as much protein, fat, and carbohydrates, or substances in food that give you energy, as most meats. They provide more nutritional fuel than fish, beans, or corn, as well as having potassium,

Would You Believe?
The two-tailed tiger swallowtail, or *llamorada*, is one of North America's largest butterflies. It was known to the Aztecs as *Xochiquetzalpapalotl* (ZOH-chi-KEHT-zahl-pah-pah-LAHT-ul) and believed to be one of the forms taken by their god.

calcium, zinc, iron, and B vitamins. Caterpillars—dried, fried, roasted, or ground into flour—fight malnutrition in many African nations. In other countries, caterpillars provide a gourmet treat. In some high-class restaurants in Mexico, a well-prepared dish of caterpillars is an expensive menu item, costing as much as $25 per plate.

People in these cultures know which butterfly larvae can be eaten and which have high levels of plant poisons. They collect the caterpillars with care, allowing a large number of caterpillars to become butterflies. This ensures future generations of caterpillars—and more high-protein meals.

The white butterflies, such as the cabbage butterfly, are thought to bring good luck.

Chapter Five

Man and Butterflies

The Karner's blue butterfly is the state butterfly of New Hampshire. It is also an endangered species. By 2001, the Karner's blue no longer flew in the Concord Pine Barrens, its only natural refuge. Since then, school children and scientists have worked together to return the Karner's blue to the wild.

Each spring, children in the Concord elementary schools grow blue lupines, the only food source for Karner's blue caterpillars. In May, they replant the lupines in the pine barrens. Captive-bred Karner's blue caterpillars are released in the protected habitat to feed and form pupae.

Recovery is a slow process. In 2005, a group of scientists counted 190 Karner's blues that survived in the wild. Another 1,300 captive-bred caterpillars were released, helping this endangered species not only survive, but also resume its place in the wild.

RECOVERY PROGRAMS

The American Zoo Association works hard to help endangered and threatened

Did You Know?
In the United States, fifteen butterfly species are currently listed as endangered or threatened, including the Bay checkerspot, Karner's blue, Lange's metalmark, and Schaus swallowtail. Of these at-risk species, nine are native to California.

butterfly species survive. These creatures are an important link in the natural food chain. Many animal species feed on butterflies throughout all four stages in the life cycle. Besides, even if they performed no function at all, butterflies are worth saving just for their beauty.

Recovery plans—programs to help save endangered species—are in place for fewer than half the at-risk butterfly

The Karner's blue butterfly is an endangered species.

species in the United States. A recovery program is a complex plan. First, scientists must identify the food sources a butterfly species prefers. The plants must be **pesticide** free so that the butterfly larvae feed, grow, and develop into adults.

Scientists must find a secure habitat in which the caterpillars can be released into the wild. Every natural habitat is filled with dangers—predators are always present and climate cannot be controlled. However, if a species is to survive it must do so in its natural environment. Across North America, zoos follow recovery plans for species native to their regions.

This western pygmy blue butterfly has a wingspan of
1 to 2 centimeters (0.39 to 0.79 inches).

Growing a Butterfly Garden

Growing a butterfly garden is a much-needed conservation project. There are 700 species of butterflies in the United States and Canada. Different species thrive in different habitats. For example, the colorful stripped policeman caterpillars feed on geraniums. A garden in the policeman's normal range should include geraniums to attract that species.

Planning a butterfly garden begins by learning what species live in or near where the garden will be placed. To attract these butterflies, simply grow the plants on which these species lay their eggs. The plants should be a rich source of nectar and flower at varying times during the spring, summer, and fall.

In the garden, avoid using chemical fertilizers, pesticides, or plant killers. These chemicals are poisons that may kill caterpillars or their larvae.

A mix of local wildflowers with varying colors should attract a wide range of butterflies. Ice plant attracts small tortoiseshells, and buddleia draws pipevine swallowtails. Flowering herbs—marjoram and oregano, for example— attract meadow browns. Grow a natural garden lush with flowers and the butterflies with come.

CONSERVATION IN ACTION

The loss of butterfly species results from several problems. Loss of habitat and extensive use of pesticides can be brought under control. Weather problems cannot.

Learning more about butterflies is one way you can help protect them.

When Hurricane Andrew swept through southern Florida in 1992, scientists thought that the entire Miami blue butterfly population had died. Luckily, a small population was discovered in 1999. Immediately, the Florida Fish and Wildlife Conservation Commission began raising Miami blues in captivity and planning release programs. Five years later, scientists released 500 Miami blue caterpillars at two of Florida's national parks. They joined the 50 or so wild Miami blues already surviving in the area. Plans to release more butterflies at ten additional sites should ensure the survival of the Miami blue species.

Butterfly exhibits have become popular zoo attractions. Through observation and education, people become more aware of ways they can help secure a future for all butterfly species. Throughout the world, public and private lands are being declared as butterfly preserves or national wilderness areas.

The National Butterfly Association supports one-day butterfly counts in the United States, Canada, and Mexico. Volunteers count the number and species of butterflies seen in an area and compare the population count to previous years. Through careful planning and preservation, these delicate insects will continue to add beauty to our lives.

Glossary

abdomen (AB-doh-mehn) the lower section of an insect body

antennae (an-TEN-nee) thin, sensory organs found on the heads of many insects

camouflage (KAM-oo-flaj) the devices that animals use to blend in with their environment

chrysalis (KRIS-uh-lihs) the pupa case of a butterfly

exoskeleton (eck-soh-SKEHL-eh-tun) a hard outer shell found on animals such as lobsters and butterfly larvae

facets (FAA-setz) the separate lenses that make up an insect's eye

larva (LAHR-vuh) wormlike life stage of insects that develop into the pupa stage; the plural is *larvae* (LAHR-vee)

metamorphosis (meht-uh-MOR-foh-sis) a complete change in body form as an animal changes into an adult

mimics (MIH-miks) copies the look or actions of another

ommatidia (ahm-uh-TIH-dee-uh) the visual facets of an insect eye

ovipositors (oh-vih-PAHZ-ih-turz) a tubular organ at the end of the abdomen of female insects and other species, used for laying eggs

pesticide (PEHS-tih-side) a poison that kills insects, rodents, and other creatures

pheromone (FAIR-uh-mohnz) a chemical substance made by an animal to attract mates or to create trails for others of the species to follow

proboscis (pro-BAH-sis) the long, flexible, tubular mouthpart of some insects

pupa (PYOO-puh) the insect stage during which an immature larva develops into an adult; the plural is *pupae* (PYOO-pee)

reproductive (ree-pro-DUK-tiv) having to do with producing young

spiracles (SPEER-uh-kulz) small openings in the side of an insect, used for breathing

thorax (THOR-aks) the middle division of an insect, crustacean, or spider

For More Information

Watch It

Butterflies, DVD. (NaritasHD, 2005.)

On the Wings of the Monarch, VHS. (Burbank, Cal.: The Dreaming Tree, 2004.)

The Story of the Butterfly, DVD. (Harrington, NJ: Janson Media, 2004.)

Read It

Carter, David. *Smithsonian Handbooks: Butterflies and Moths.* New York: Dorling Kindersley Publishing, 2002.

Hunt, Joni Phelps. *A Shimmer of Butterflies.* Montrose, Calif: London Town Press, 2005.

McEvey, Shane F. *Moths and Butterflies.* Broomall, Penn.: Chelsea House Publications, 2001.

Preston-Mafham, Ken. *The Secret World of Butterflies and Moths.* Chicago: Raintree Publishing, 2002.

World Book. *Monarchs and Other Butterflies.* Chicago: World Book, Inc., 2005.

Look It Up

Visit our Web site for lots of links about butterflies: *http://www.childsworld.com/links*

Note to Parents, Teachers, and Librarians: We routinely verify our Web links to make sure they are safe, active sites—so encourage your readers to check them out!

The Animal Kingdom
Where Do Butterflies Fit In?

Kingdom: Animalia

Phylum: Arthropoda

Class: Insecta

Order: Lepidoptera

Genus and Species: 18,000 or more butterfly species

Relatives: caddisflies

Index

About the Author
Sophie Lockwood is a former teacher and a longtime writer. She writes textbooks, newspaper articles, and magazine articles. Sophie enjoys writing about animals and their habits. The most interesting part of her research, Sophie says, is learning how scientists apply their knowledge to save endangered species. She lives with her husband in the foothills of the Blue Ridge Mountains.